# TIPS & TOOLS

FOR

STUDENT SUCCESS

By Sue Paulson

Copyright © 1999 by Sue Paulson. All rights reserved.

Published by Fingertip Solutions.

No part of this work may be reproduced or transmitted in any form or by any means, electronic or mechanical, including photocopying and recording, or by any information storage or retrieval system without the prior permission of Fingertip Solutions unless such copying is expressly permitted by federal copyright law. For permission, please write to Fingertip Solutions, 1081 Parker Drive, Sherwood Park, Alberta, Canada T8A 1C7

Every effort has been made to credit sources. Any errors will be corrected in future additions.

Printed and bound in Canada

Cover Design & Illustrations:Jason Wieler

Desktop Publishing: Deb Dedla

Clipart: CorelDraw v. 8

ISBN: 1-894393-00-7

For bulk rates or to order additional copies, contact:

Fingertip Solutions

Fax: (780) 417-3181
E-mail: coaches@edmc.net

This book is dedicated to all students for whom lifelong learning is the route to lifelong success.

ACKNOWLEDGMENTS

Two very special friends inspired this book. Doreen Davison, my mentor and colleague, introduced me to the joys and challenges of teaching student success strategies. Together we have coached and coaxed many classes to new heights of achievement. Lorne Gold, entrepreneur and madcap inventor, generously gave his pocket-sized concept to me and spurred me on with a kick-in-the-butt or a fresh idea.

No one creates anything without support from loved ones. George Ward, my dad, showed me how to be tenacious and courageous. My husband, Clare, and son, Trevor, provided love, encouragement, and hot meals.

To Ian Hay for his backing and enthusiasm. Deb Dedla, for her patience and hard work in formatting, Jason Wieler for his lively and fun illustrations, Thomas Wharton for editing comments, Sue Smith and Connie Warner for reviewing the rough draft and to countless others who gave so generously of their time and expertise – my heartfelt thanks. I couldn't have done it without you.

THE SYMBOLS ARE YOUR GUIDE!

Throughout each chapter, information has been divided into Tips and Tools.

To find **TIPS**, look for the following icon:

To search for **TOOLS**, watch for this sign:

Table of Contents

		Page
	Introduction	IX
Chapter 1:	Attitudes & Behaviors	1
Chapter 2:	Habits	9
Chapter 3:	Creative & Critical Thinking	15
Chapter 4:	Time Mastery	25
Chapter 5:	Reading	33
Chapter 6:	Note Taking	43
Chapter 7:	Memory	63
Chapter 8:	Exam Preparation	73
Chapter 9:	Writing	81
Chapter 10:	Balance	89
	Bibliography	97

INTRODUCTION

"Though no one can go back and make a brand new start, anyone can start from now and make a brand new ending."
Carl Bard

When I first started teaching study skills, I was thrilled to discover the wealth of material available to make learning easier. This in-depth information made a huge difference in my students' grades and lives, but was only available in a time-consuming, textbook format.

If you're like me and have limited time and/or resources and a similar need to do well with ongoing studies, then this pocket-size selection of the most effective tips and tools will be invaluable.

Tips & Tools for Student Success was created to provide a quick reference guide to help you improve your study skills and succeed, regardless of course content.

Whether your goal is to get straight A's on your way to a degree, or to simply pass your most difficult subject, plan now to use the ideas in this book to create the most positive learning environment you can.

My students have succeeded. You can too!

Sue Paulson

CHAPTER 1

ATTITUDES AND BEHAVIORS

"The greatest discovery of my generation is that human beings, by changing the inner attitudes of their minds, can change the outer aspects of their lives."

William James

ATTITUDES AND BEHAVIORS

A learning mind set begins with seeing yourself as successful, regardless of the obstacles.

Napolean Hill, in his book *Think and Grow Rich,* once said:

"What the mind of man can conceive and believe, it can achieve."

Your challenge is to use Hill's wisdom for your benefit. Use the tips and tools in this chapter to re-program your thinking about current school experiences. Fears and failures from the past can still influence you now unless you change the way you see yourself.

For example, my problems with math in grade seven helped create a "give-up" mentality that followed me all the way through high school.

Refuse to let those old pictures ruin your current experience. You'll be far more effective in class if you don't take all that old baggage with you.

Both the Visualization and the Affirmations tools in this chapter will help you move beyond the past.

Mood changes sway our thinking. Experiment with ways to switch out of the negative and into a positive focus. Try laughter - laughing helps us think more broadly and associate more freely.

VISUALIZATION

Have a pen and paper close by. To begin to create success in your studies, start with the following visualization:

❶ Find a comfortable chair in a quiet place. Sit upright with hands in your lap and feet flat on the floor. Close your eyes, take a deep breath, and as you exhale, imagine your whole body relaxing. Keep breathing deeply for another minute as you focus on relaxing your body and mind.

❷ Keep your eyes closed and imagine that you are sitting in front of a large blank movie screen. Lights come on, the camera rolls and you see yourself on screen - working in class, studying well, passing your exams and finally, walking on stage, in cap and gown, to receive your diploma. You made it, you're a success! Pay attention to all the details of this scene - how you looked, where you were, and who was there. It's also important to notice and feel any emotions from this scene. When this image of success is locked in, allow the screen to fade, take a couple more deep breaths, and open your eyes.

❸ Immediately write down what you saw and felt. Post this image on the wall in your study area.

Whenever you feel overwhelmed or anxious about yourself or your studies, read over your experience from the visualization. Take time to remember how it felt to be successful. This reminder will help re-focus your energies.

ATTITUDE ADJUSTMENT

"The more prone to worry a person is, the poorer their academic performance."

Daniel Goleman
Author of Emotional Intelligence

Everyone brings old fears, beliefs and attitudes about school to new study situations. If you take time to examine these old notions, most will no longer apply. At the very least, by now you have developed many coping resources that offset any negative history.

On a sheet of paper, write a list of all those old fears and beliefs (e.g. "I'm lousy at math, I can't do tests, I'll never be a success" etc.) Now examine this list one by one. Place a star beside the items you think are still true today. (Some of these were likely never true.)

Replace any thoughts that don't apply to you today with positive statements, commonly called affirmations.
e.g. "I'll never be a success" might change to "I am successful in all my classes."

With each of the items you starred as still true, list some ideas for overcoming those challenges. Then act on those ideas, step by step.

Affirmations are a great way to help you change a negative thought to a positive one. To be of benefit...they must be worded in the present, as if they have already happened.
e.g. I am an "A" student, or I am successful in all my classes.

NOTES

CHAPTER 2

HABITS

"The unfortunate thing about this world is that the good habits are much easier to give up than the bad ones."

W. Somerset Maugham

HABITS

A habit is simply a behaviour that's repeated over and over until it becomes part of the way we do things. Habits can be our masters or slaves, weapons against us, or tools to help us.

Unfortunately, most of my students have the same favorite study habit that I do - **procrastination**! Working best to deadlines can be productive, but 3:00 a.m. the day that paper is due is a bit extreme. When procrastination becomes a habit, then it's a problem.

Following are some success habits that students recommend:

☞ *Restrict t.v. and telephone time and use as rewards for completion of study goals.*

☞ *Study in a quiet area, free of distractions.*

☞ *Re-structure your time with school as the major priority.*

☞ *Participate in a study group.*

Be realistic when creating new habit patterns. Change only one habit at a time.

HABIT CHANGE

❶ Make a list of all your study habits. Sort them into two columns - Success Habits and Barriers to Success. Now pick one item from your Barriers list that's important to change.

Decide what you will do differently, and write an affirmation about it. (e.g. To overcome poor memory you've decided to create time each day to review every subject. Your affirmation might read: *"Every day I spend 30 minutes reviewing class notes."*)

❷ Now follow through. Commit daily to the new habit by reading your affirmation and doing what you said you'd do.

At the end of the week, measure your progress and reward yourself for each achievement. If you have poor results, check that your goal is realistic, make any adjustments, then re-commit for the next week.

When you decide to change or add any habit, focus on it daily for one month. Assess your progress. If you are satisfied, then pick a second habit to change and work with that one for another 30 days.

NOTES

CHAPTER 3

CREATIVE & CRITICAL THINKING

"The depth of your relaxation, your ability to let go, determines the height of your creativity."

            Dr. Harold Cooper (qtd. in Simpson 251)

CREATIVE THINKING

Were you one of those kids who was constantly chastised for daydreaming? Albert Einstein, one of the most creative minds of our time, was labeled a "dummy" by many of his teachers. It's a good thing for us he didn't believe them!

A lot of our creative power is accessed when we allow our minds to dream and envision. All inventions come from this creative part of our thinking process and has only the limits we set for it.

Think about the number of goods and services in our society. They all started as creative ideas.

Creative thinking can also be used to solve problems. The more options you can create, the better your chances to find the best answer.

A good friend once said that there are at least 10 solutions to every problem. Whenever you're stuck in a challenge and need some answers, try the brainstorming tool.

Use brainstorming to generate topic ideas for group projects, presentations, and essays.

The collective power of group brainstorming can make the impossible - possible!

BRAINSTORMING

Brainstorming is a great way to generate many ideas and solutions.

<u>Rules of Brainstorming</u>

1. Set a goal for the number of items desired. (e.g. 10 solutions, 20 ideas)

2. List all ideas, no matter how wild.

3. Don't allow any criticism of ideas.

Once you have your list, start reducing it by connecting similar ideas and grouping them under headings.

For group brainstorming, give each person post-it notes. Everyone writes just one idea per note, then sticks all their notes to a large sheet or board.

Choose a coordinator to sort and group the notes. Duplicate ideas are eliminated. The remaining ones can then be placed in order of importance.

Corel Clipart

CRITICAL THINKING

Critical thinking is defined as "thorough thinking".*(Ellis 204)* Anytime you analyze before making a decision, you are thinking critically.

Good critical thinkers look carefully at all sides of an issue in order to make informed decisions. They refuse to agree with others without first examining proof, actions, and the end results.

Every day life presents us with many opportunities to think critically - should you buy a car or take the bus - go to work or go back to school. Start now to sharpen your ability to use reason and logic.

QUESTIONING

When gathering information about any topic, it's important to know what is opinion and what is fact. Facts can be supported by evidence, while opinions cannot. Questioning will help sort these differences out.

1. What information (statistics, figures, examples) will prove or support your main idea, issue, or premise?

2. If it's a belief or point of view, what is it based on and what is the opposite argument?

Once you've done this research, it's a lot easier to develop a point of view and expand on it. Your instructors will quickly poke holes in any unsupported position. If you find those holes first and fix them, better grades will follow.

◌⊸ **Use critical thinking to test assumptions about what you know.**

An assumption is a belief or idea that you take for granted without always having proof that it is true. Before Christopher Columbus, people thought the world was flat! Be willing to change your assumptions based on new evidence.

e.g. You assume you know the content of a test because your study partner told you what the instructor said. A closer look at the exam will prove or disprove this assumption.
Maybe you better talk to the teacher yourself!

NOTES

CHAPTER 4

TIME MASTERY

"Get the most done, in the least time, with the best results - work smart, not hard!"

Unknown

TIME MASTERY

GOAL OF TIME MASTERY

"Hard work that is focused creates its own momentum."

Stockwell Day (CHED interview)

College or university life demands a minimum of 1 - 2 hours of homework time for every hour spent in the classroom. Most of my students moan that they have no life beyond school. It's especially challenging for those with a family and/or a job to add to the equation.

Don't despair - there is help! Those who develop the ability to prioritize and manage their activities are destined to succeed. Test out the ideas in this chapter to find ways to make time work for you.

Corel Clipart

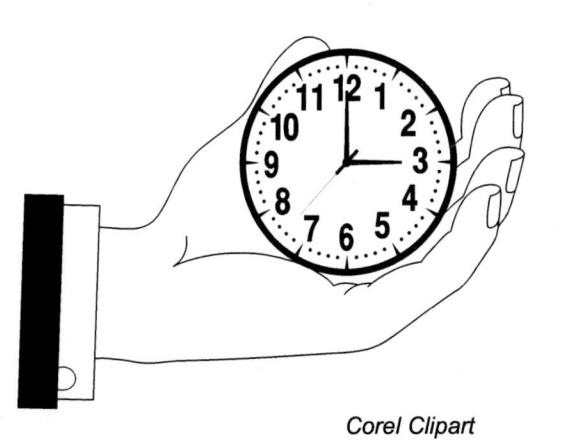

TIME LOG

❶ In 15 - 30 minute intervals, track your daily activities on a time log for one week. After seven days, review your log. Pay attention to time wasters and habits that sabotage your achievement efforts.

❷ Now set up a one-week activity plan that will help you meet your goals and deadlines. Then follow your plan. (Remember to build in some relaxation time.)

❸ At the end of that week, analyze how well you did.

❹ Adjust your schedule, and try again for another week.

Reward yourself for every success in managing your time.

DAILY PLANNER

"Procrastination is the art of keeping up with yesterday."

Don Marquis

If you struggle to remember all your activities and appointments, then you need a daily planner to help you keep on time and on track!

The most common choices are daily, weekly and monthly planners. Some schools and colleges provide them free at the beginning of the school year.

Decide which type suits you best, then get in the habit of carrying it everywhere and using it daily. Schedule study times, exams, assignment deadlines, and of course, the rest of your life.

Be sure to leave periods of time open for emergencies and the unexpected!

When Planning Study Time:

☞ Set priorities.

☞ Give more time to core/difficult subjects.

☞ Choose your best time of day to study tedious/difficult material.

☞ Break study time into small, workable chunks.

☞ Reward yourself with a 5 - 10 minute break when your study goal is achieved.

When Planning Chores and Errands:

☞ Combine tasks whenever possible. (E.g. write grocery list in bank line-up)

☞ Plan your route for errands to cut down on travel time.

☞ To reduce your cleaning time at home, do a daily 10-minute pick-up.

NOTES

CHAPTER 5

READING

"Reading is a means of thinking with another person's mind; it forces you to stretch your own."

Charles Scribner Jr (qtd. In Simpson 388)

READING

Reading textbooks effectively is a very different skill from reading for pleasure. The goal of textbook reading is to make sure you understand the material and know where to find answers to questions.

Authors and editors of text books work very hard to provide students with solid information in a useful format.

Time spent getting to know your books will be rewarded, both during class and at exam time.

Before classes even start, get to know your textbooks. Flip through very quickly, from cover to cover. Pay attention to the set up:

1. Is there a chapter summary?
2. How long are the chapters?
3. What kinds of information does the book cover?
4. What extra resources are in the back of the text?

HIGHLIGHTS

There are three different ways to make important information stand out in your texts:

> Highlight
> Underline
> Annotate

Both highlighting and underlining serve the same purpose - they provide memory cues that help with review.

Test out the different colors of highlighters to find your favorite. A regular ballpoint pen is best for underlining. Regardless of which method you use, don't mark more than 10% of any page of text.

Annotating is simply making notes in the margins of your text. This helps improve your concentration while reading (to prevent dozing off!) and will trigger new thoughts for your notes.

**Read with a dictionary beside you.
Either underline words to look up later, or
look them up as you read.**

CODES

As you read, some words and concepts will have similar meaning or a similar purpose. Create a shorthand code for future notes that could include one or more of the following: circles, boxes, and underlines.

Note how this is done in the following paragraphs:

Code: underline - subjects
        circle - names
        box - dates

Mathematics can be separated into five different subjects: <u>arithmetic</u>, <u>algebra</u>, <u>geometry</u>, <u>trigonometry</u>, and <u>calculus.</u> While almost everyone does simple arithmetic, about 40 percent of the population use one or more of the other subjects.

Archimedes (287 - 212 BC) produced several books in geometry, while three of the Bernoulli brothers from Switzerland (1623 - 1807) contributed to the development and application of calculus. Carl Gauss (1777 - 1855) was the greatest mathematician of the early 19th century. Much of his work was in the field of mathematical physics. *(Vol. Library 2 1513)*

READING SPEEDS

Skimming - read <u>key</u> parts at normal speed, skip the rest.

✓ Use skimming to locate new material, to get a general idea, to find specific references, or to review

Rapid - read everything on the page as quickly as you can

✓ Use rapid reading to get to the main idea or Central plot, to review familiar material, or to read for pleasure

Normal - read at your usual pace

✓ Use normal reading to draw attention to details, to understand how details relate to the main idea, or to appreciate the literary style

Careful - read thoroughly, at a slow pace

✓ Use careful reading to master content, evaluate material, or analyze.

For all assigned reading, take the first five minutes to skim the chapter. As you quickly turn the pages, read the title, then just the first paragraph. Read headings, captions of diagrams, and the conclusion or last paragraph. If the chapter has a quiz at the end, skim those questions.
Reading this information out loud will help lock in the general concepts even better.

NOTES

CHAPTER 6

NOTE TAKING

"Good intentions are no substitute for actions; failure usually follows the path of least persistence."

                                    Unknown

NOTE TAKING

Taking notes from your texts and from class lectures will be easier if you understand what the purpose of the course is and the purpose or major learning from each chapter.

As you preview each chapter and section, look for the major learning goal. This information will help you decide what kind of notes to take.

When in doubt, show your notes to the instructor to get feedback about content and accuracy. You can also check notes with a classmate to confirm your learning.

Test out as many different ways of taking notes as you can so you can discover which tools work best for you.

Remember that everyone will have different methods based on individual learning style.

COMPONENTS OF ALL INFORMATION

Most information will have two components:

> Statements - concepts, points of view
>
> PIE - pieces to back up the statements
>
> > **P**roof
> > **I**nformation
> > **E**xamples

Pay attention to how the information sorts itself out. It will either fit into one of the above categories or will form a connection with other data. *(Hanau 16)*

While it may not always be efficient or practical to assess information this way, by practicing this tool, you will soon improve your sorting ability.

The following paragraph is a good example of a concept that has enough PIE to make it easy to understand:

Photosynthesis is a form of energy conversion. It occurs in green plants when the energy of light captures carbon dioxide molecules from the air and reduces them to energy in the form of sugar. This process nourishes the plant, which in turn supports all others higher on the food chain. An apple tree supplies fruit, fuel (its wood), and most important, oxygenated air.
                        Eg. *(Volume Library 2 1909)*

In the preceding paragraph, sentence one states the concept, sentence two provides proof, sentence three gives information, and sentence four relates an example.

Corel Clipart

TEXTBOOK NOTES

Hunt for as many pieces of PIE as you can to understand the concepts and main ideas.

LECTURE NOTES

Sit in the front rows and pay close attention to your instructor.

Using repetition, emphasis, tone of voice, key questions, examples, and terms & definitions, instructors will signal important points – often potential exam questions. (Carter et al. 202)

Copy all lists or outlines from the board. In both the first and last five minutes of the lecture, write down everything the instructor says. Use the categories your teacher gives you.

Write down your information as fast as you can, without concern for organization. Set aside extra time for fixing and organizing within 24 hours of that lecture.

To write faster when taking lecture notes, use a personal shorthand to abbreviate words. Only jot down key points and forget about correct spelling.

Translate your notes as quickly as you can after class.

REVIEW METHODS

There are several different ways to organize and review material for exams.

1. **Concept Maps** - Concept maps start with a general idea or topic, then add more specific details and components. This visual can show connections between material that you might not see in your notes.

Print the main idea or topic in the middle of your page. Draw a circle or square around it. Then, using lines and other circles or squares, add all the supporting data that connects to the main topic. The supporting points are drawn in random, not sequential order.

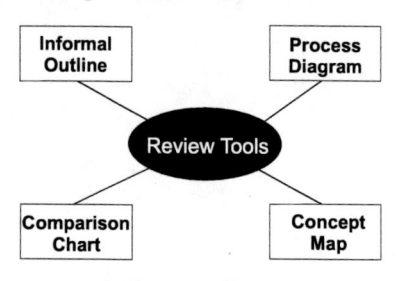

```
  Informal                Process
  Outline                 Diagram
        \               /
         \             /
          Review Tools
         /             \
        /               \
  Comparison            Concept
    Chart                 Map
```

2. **Comparison Charts** - Whenever you need to compare or contrast any information, create a chart that helps you reorganize key points.

Types of Foods		
Kinds	Benefit	Daily Servings
meat	protein	1-3
fruit	vitamins	4-6
grains	fibre	3-5

3. **Time Lines** - To help remember important dates and supporting points, draw a time line. This sequential visual helps your brain to lock in history notes and any other time-related material.

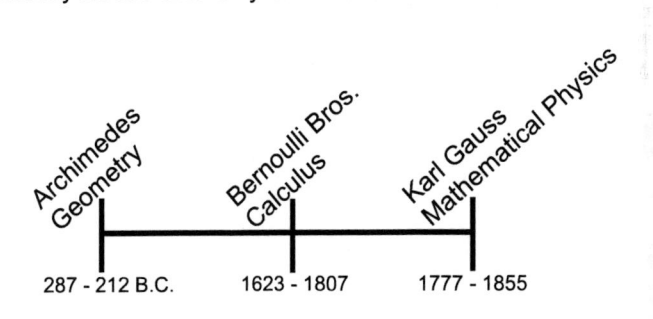

Archimedes Geometry	Bernoulli Bros. Calculus	Karl Gauss Mathematical Physics
287 - 212 B.C.	1623 - 1807	1777 - 1855

4. **Process Diagrams** - processes are methods, steps and stages that describe how things happen. A diagram that clearly shows these processes will make learning and remembering easier.

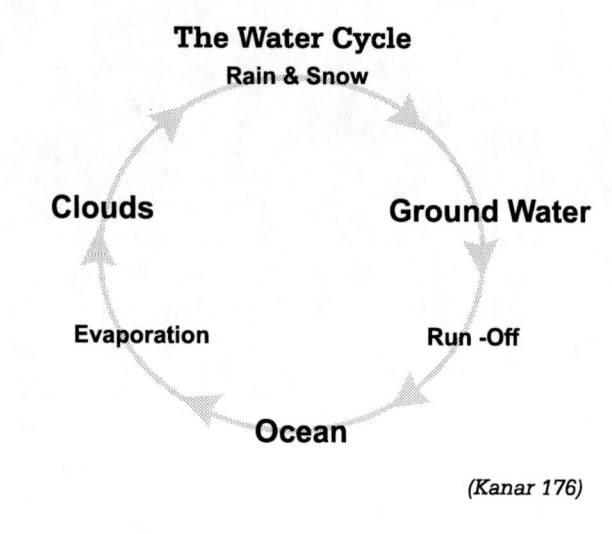

The Water Cycle

- Rain & Snow
- Clouds
- Ground Water
- Evaporation
- Run-Off
- Ocean

(Kanar 176)

If you are a visual learner, use time lines, process diagrams, and concept maps to help you "see" and remember the information more easily. Experiment with colored markers or colored paper to make certain items stand out.

5. **Informal Outlines** - An informal outline plots key ideas in a very organized way. Using a lettering and numbering system, information is sorted into main headings and supporting points. Remember to indent each new subsection.

A. Main idea
- a. supporting points
- b.   "
- c.   "

B. Main idea
- a. supporting points
    - i. supports (a)
    - ii.   "
    - iii. "
- b.
- c.

Label, number and date all notes. Also include the page numbers from your texts. The more organized your notes are, the easier your review time will be.

Write your name and phone number on notebooks in case they get lost or misplaced.

6. **Cornell Method** - This method sorts facts on a single page. Simply draw a vertical line about 2 inches (5 cm) from the left edge of your page, creating a margin. This space is used for key words or ideas. The right side provides the details or explanations.

(Ellis 127)

If your information can be sorted into any of the following four categories, then use this method:

Date	What happened
Formula	Uses, Examples
Word	Definition
Concept	How to apply

Type some or all of your hand-written notes. Not only will they take less space, this task gives you another chance to review the material and spot missing pieces.

(Ellis 133)

Use a larger font and double-space the lines to make these notes easier to read.

INDEX CARDS

Also known as recipe cards or 3 X 5 cards, this handy tool comes in packages of 100 or in a perforated, coil- bound booklet. Choose the size & color you prefer.

(Ellis 149)

Many students use them as flash cards.

Side One	Side Two
Questions or	Answers
Formulas or	Definitions & examples
Words or	Meanings & Uses
Dates	Facts about dates

You can also draw your concept maps and comparison charts on these.

To use your cards for quick review when riding the bus, waiting in line, walking to class, or reviewing in a study group, hole punch the upper left corner of each card, then use a split ring to hold them together.

(The student who shared this idea used it to move his grades from "C's" to "A's".)

NOTES

CHAPTER 7

MEMORY

"No memory is ever alone; it's at the end of a trail of memories, a dozen trails that each have their own associations."

Louis L'Amour
(Ride the River)

MEMORY

Much like the functioning of a computer, our memory serves as an information processor. When we receive or take in information, we decide whether to store it or discard it.

RETENTION is the name used for storing data. All data needs to move quickly from our short term memory to long term memory, in order to retain it.

RECALL is the term we use to bring back or remember what was learned or stored.

RECALLING what you learned is a crucial skill around exam time. Both your reading and note taking abilities play key roles in locking in and remembering material. Use all the tools from chapters 5 & 6 to help your memory.

Do all homework assignments. The extra practice with new concepts or procedures will help with retention.

(Maureen, a student of mine, used this tip to score an "A" on her Anthropology exam.)

REPETITION AND RECITATION

REVIEW all lecture notes within 24 hours to move this information from short term to long term memory. The more often you review newly-stored information, the faster you can bring it back.

RECITE out loud to improve retention - once you've learned a concept, recite it five more times to lock it in. Use your own words - it's easier to remember your own words than someone else's.

You can also improve your memory by teaching what you learn to someone else.

To remember large amounts of information, never do the same thing with the same material <u>twice</u>. For example, re-learn from existing notes by creating concept maps. Then teach this information to someone else or recite it out loud. The more senses you use, the more paths of recall you open up.

SHORT BLOCKS OF TIME

Divide your notes into smaller sections that can be easily reviewed in short time frames.

Research shows that we remember the first and last of what we study more easily than the middle part. If your study session is too long, much of your review will be forgotten.

More frequent bursts of concentrated studying yield much better results on tests and prevent burnout. So schedule short time frames (10 - 20 min.), and divide your notes into smaller sections for easy review. Be sure to take a 5 minute break between each section.

Do something fun or relaxing on your short breaks, as both a reward for your hard work and a way of re-charging your mind and body.

Eg. A quick phone call to a friend, a short computer game, or even a power nap will generate energy.

REVIEW STEPS

<u>Daily Review</u> - organize and review new material within 24 hrs. of lecture (5-10 min./subject)

<u>Weekly Review</u> - at the end of the week, spend 30 min. - 1 hr./subject reviewing what you learned that week.

<u>Exam Review</u> - 7-10 days before exams, block off larger chunks of time to cover all the information.

(Ellis 148)

"Cramming" is the least effective way to remember material.

However, if you must cram:

- plan your time

- carefully choose what to cram

- set deadlines for learning

- recite notes over and over and over

- RELAX!

NOTES

CHAPTER 8

EXAM PREPARATION

"Experience is a hard teacher because she gives the test first, the lesson afterwards."
Vernon Sanders Law

EXAM PREPARATION

Test results are <u>not</u> an indication of intelligence level. They simply provide feedback about how well you know that material.

All the work you do in any subject prior to your midterm or final helps prepare you for that exam.

Get organized by mapping out a study schedule that starts at least a week before mid-terms or finals. Be sure to build in a few fun activities to re-energize and relieve the stress of studying.

Re-read the Note-taking chapter for review tips and tools.

Canadian author, Thomas Wharton, suggests recording your notes on tape, then playing them back while doing chores or traveling to and from campus.

PHYSICAL READINESS

Before Exams:

The night before - pack everything you'll need - pens, pencils, erasers, calculator, water bottle.

Get a good night's sleep.

The Day of the Exam:

Arrive on time or even 5 minutes early.

Listen carefully to any verbal instructions.

Skim the whole exam first and notice how marks are assigned.

Plan your timing for each section.

Read all instructions very carefully and underline key words or questions.

Answer the easiest questions first.

Guessing Strategies for Multiple Choice Tests

If there is no penalty for guessing and you don't know the answer to some of the multiple choice, then guess!

1. Any multiple choice option that has the following words in its statement - all, always or never - is often an incorrect answer.

2. The more familiar an option is to you, the more likely it's the right one.

3. If the list of options is a list of numbers, middle numbers tend to be correct answers,

MENTAL PREPARATION

To reduce anxiety and worry, remember to breathe! Deep, slow breathing sends a signal to the brain to relax.

Visualize success - the night before each exam, take a few moments to calm yourself, close your eyes, and visualize the success you want. In your mind's eye, see the desired grade already achieved.

If you find yourself worrying or dwelling on disaster, do something physical to distract your mind. Exercise will trigger endorphins - nature's mood-lifting substance.

!

Include rough notes and/or outlines for essay questions. Even if you run out of time, you may get some marks for that draft.

NOTES

CHAPTER 9

WRITING

"The force is within you. Force yourself."
                                    Harrison Ford

Corel Clipart

WRITING

Our computer age has added significantly to the need for well-crafted, written communication.

The business community insists on clear, precise language that is error-free. Academic papers are rigorously checked for content, accuracy and proof.

To prepare you for these expectations, written assignments are a big component of many school subjects. With practice, you can communicate your research, thoughts, and ideas in a clear, logical manner that will earn you high marks. A portion of the writing process will include the creative and critical thinking skills from Chapter 3.

FREE WRITING

That all-important essay is due next week and you have the dreaded writer's block! Try free writing.

Free writing is the process of writing any words you want without pausing or stopping to make corrections. Even if all you write is your name, over and over, that physical involvement puts the brain into gear, which is much more effective than staring at the blank page or screen.

As you start, give yourself permission to write the worst garbage you can imagine. Remember that the best writers throw out more words than they use.

To exercise your free-writing muscles, use either pen and paper, or the computer. Pick any topic, set a timer for five minutes, then start. <u>Don't stop</u> to think. <u>Don't stop</u> to correct anything. Just keep writing until your time is up. Once you've mastered the first five minutes, try for ten.

It's a good idea to put the first draft of your essay or report in a drawer for a couple of days. Then when you take it out to edit, mistakes will be easier to spot.

Be sure to leave plenty of time in your schedule for re-writing and editing.

WRITING ESSAYS

When writing short essays, try using a Five-Paragraph Plan:

Paragraph 1   Introduction of topic

Paragraph 2,3 & 4   One main point/paragraph with evidence to support the topic

Paragraph 5   Conclusion and implications for the reader
(Kanar 335)

This plan makes it easier to sort your research notes and write the paper in a more organized way.

Start writing your first draft at whatever point is easiest for you. Some students start with an outline and begin at the beginning. Others write the ending first. Experiment with what works for you, then do it.

NOTES

CHAPTER 10

BALANCE

"Stress is the key to excellence -- when you know how to manage it."
Peter G. Hanson, M.D.

Corel Clipart

BALANCE

Stress can build up very quickly when you try to balance learning with daily living. It's important to know which strategies will help reduce the negative effects of stress.

Five different coping resources will also contribute to your ability to maintain a balance:

> Satisfaction Level
> Problem-solving Ability
> Communication Skills
> Closeness to Others
> Flexibility

The better developed your coping resources are, the less stress will bother you.

MANAGING STRESS

Two areas that you can work with to minimize the negative effects of stress are nutrition and physical fitness.

Nutrition: Our brains tend to work better with regular, nourishing food and lots of water. Many students deplete their energies and increase their stress with hurried meals of fast and/or junk food and an over consumption of salt, sugar, and caffeine.

Plan for and pack healthy snacks for breaks throughout the day. Limit caffeine to 1 or 2 cups/day. Increase your water intake to 6 - 8 glasses/day.

Physical Fitness: The body was meant to move. A brisk 20 min. walk after a heavy class or study time restores energy and a state of calmness. Any aerobic activity that you enjoy and lasts for at least 20 minutes will be beneficial.

Meditation or guided visualization is also very helpful in re-charging the body. Add a soothing nature tape, like ocean waves, for even better results.

Use music as a healing tool. Play your favorite relaxing music when you need to calm down, or something lively when you need a boost.

SUPPORT SYSTEMS

Whether you are a returning student after many years or have just graduated junior or senior high school, you will need a strong support system to help you succeed. Who can you turn to who supports you in reaching your goals?

Make a list of those you know who can fill the following roles in your life:

mentors and advisors

cheerleaders and celebrators

study buddies

financial supporters

Often, instructors, parents, spouses and friends will fill many of these roles. The more people you have building you up and cheering you on, the easier it will be for you to do your job.

Laughter in your day is as important as food. The more often you can laugh with others and at yourself, the more you can de-stress your life.

Particularly at exam time, find some carefree activities that are good for a giggle. Cartoons or comedy videos are great outlets for stress release.

NOTES

Bibliography

Carter, Carol. et al., *Keys to Success*. Cnd.ed. Scarborough, ON: Prentice 1998. 202

Ellis, David. *Becoming a Master Student*. 2nd Cnd. ed. USA: Houghton 1997. 127,130,133, 148, 149, 167, 204

Hanau, Laia. *Play the Study Game for Better Grades*. 5th ed. New York: Barnes 1985. 16

Hanson, Peter G. *Stress for Success*. Toronto, ON: Collins 1989.

Kanar, Carol C. *The Confident Student*. 3rd ed. Boston: Houghton 1998. 176, 335

Simpson, James B. *Simpson's Contemporary Quotations*. Rev. ed. USA: HarperCollins 1997. 251, 388

The Volume Library 2. Nashville: Southwestern 1993. 1513 - 1516, 1909

About The Author

After 12 years in corporate training, Sue started teaching public speaking, business writing, and study skills at two Edmonton colleges.

Tips & Tools for Student Success is her first book. Between teaching and speaking assignments, she writes fantasy novels for young adults.

Sue lives in Sherwood Park, Alberta with her husband, son, two cats and a salamander.

WORKSHOPS

Fingertip Solutions have developed customized workshops suitable for both part-time and full-time students.

These workshops demonstrate the tools that are important to student success, and are tailored to the needs of each group.

Enable your students to learn the valuable skills needed to become **SUCCESSFUL STUDENTS!**

For more information or to book your customized workshop, contact:

FINGERTIP SOLUTIONS
Phone: 1-780-449-6633
Fax: 1-780-417-3181
Email: coaches@edmc.net

ORDER FORM

Visit your local bookstore for additional copies of Tips & Tools for *Student Success,* or fill out the following order form and enclose a cheque or money order.

	Quantity	Price (+GST)	Total

Tips & Tools for
Student Success _____ x $ 9.95 = _____

*Shipping: Please add $ 3.00/first book,
       $ 1.50/each book thereafter*   + _____

GST: 7% of total of book + shipping   + _____
(Also add applicable provincial tax)

Total Order = _____

Name: _____

Address: _____

City: _____

Province: _____ *Postal Code:* _____

Please mail to: Fingertip Solutions, 1081 Parker Dr., Sherwood Park, AB T8A 1C7.